31143009261562
811.54 Lipton
Lipton, Robert, 1959-
A complex bravery : poems

Y0-BSC-343

A COMPLEX
BRAVERY

DISCARDED
RICHMOND PUBLIC LIBRAR

Library of Congress Cataloging in Publication Data

Lipton, Robert, 1959-
A Complex Bravery.
Poems in English
ISBN 0-9712676-1-8

Copyright © Robert Lipton, 2006
Edited by Halli Villegas
Design and typesetting by Sean Tai
Cover design by Sean Tai and Halli Villegas
Copyediting by Myna Wallin
Cover photo by David Bigham

Printed and bound in Canada

Marick Press
P.O. Box 36253
Grosse Pointe Farms
Michigan 48236
www.marickpress.com

A COMPLEX BRAVERY

poems by

ROBERT LIPTON

MARICK
PRESS

Toronto • Detroit

To my parents who gave me no choice

Once a writer is born into a family, that family is doomed
– Czeslaw Milosz

CONTENTS

There will be trees with vines painted
on the walls directly in front of the cage
so as to direct the baby's attention, the other
walls will be beige and feature the thinnest
palimpsest of biblical events, Abraham
about to slay his son, Job looking over
a field of dead cows, to guide the baby's
dreams a Geiger counter will mark changes
in the earth's radioactive core directly below
the baby's cage, shifts in gravity within 0.5
meters of the cage will be used as a surrogate
for appropriate mental hygiene, a tray of ripe
tropical fruit, in season, will be brought
almost within arm's length of the cage door
construction sounds will be piped in and as puberty
comes a window will be painted onto the left
wall showing an open plain interspersed with oak
trees and in the magic light of late afternoon
the lengthened, watery shadow
of a woman with outstretched hands
slanting across the field of view
in apparent aspect, substantial and 50 yards across.

POOL BOY

My skin feels full of liquid
like a drowning victim
or like always being 17
in my parent's kitchen
hamburger helper set to simmer
the Mexican maid silent with rage
breasts pushing out the side of her halter.
Mom searches for her Vicodin
the sister with mummy arms
rushes away.

Our pool is painted black
the tile a copy from the Minoan
porpoises dancing in heavy seas.
Sun flashes against the
gray aluminum of my net
near the Jacuzzi.
I skim the summer insects
and dyed hair from the water
a smile catches in the
surface tension.

HEROICS

His eyes rolled to the side,
he has exceptionally big eyes
and you could see
a lot of white, crazy white,
so I noticed the white,
the ease of his normally drum-tight
mouth and missed the thing
about the line of Police
snipers sneaking up the stairs,
the heavy fog of marijuana
smoke like a comforter
kept me in the curve
of the futon couch.
I glanced back at the TV
with the illegal cable box
which obscured the 20,000 dollars
of freshly-harvested weed
glistening in the Steuben crystal pitcher,
caught myself wondering about the severity
of the fine for dicking with cable,
telling my brother it was just the local
crows playing with the fat tabby;
the crows knock against the aluminum
siding force the cat to skid its butt
against the planters lined up
like congregants waiting for communion.

The shadows against the curtain
were blocky and moved slowly
as if creatures from Mercury
had been beamed to our walkway.
I told him these actually were creatures
from Mercury and not to worry
the crows would take care of them, too.
My brother sat down with his hands
resting on his open legs, palms up.
He was waiting like a submariner Buddha
for the depth charges to explode,
his eyes moving in slow circles
like sonar or a permanently
wizened vaudevillian.
I was tense, too,
waiting for the line of pizza
delivery boys to finally figure out
where I lived and get up the nerve
to muscle through the heavy blokes
from Mercury, paradoxically
moving like glaciers.

TEENAGE

We had kittens
and large noble gas-filled balloons.
We would tie the balloons
with hemp twine
to the hind legs of each
kitten and release the completed
unit at sundown when the
sun bejeweled the balloons.
We watched
as long as we could
drinking beer
not catching anyone's eye.

DELIVERY

Your laughter with your lover
in the room across the plains of the den,
the call of hyenas when a zebra stumbles,
the little "I love you's" plastered on my skin
atomized into the smell of cordite.

I ready myself in a low
crouch behind the nubuck lounger.
I will engage (close) with force
answer only to my name,
smile as if seen through a
rifle sight.

I eat with my hands and rush
the second floor —
this battle is parent by parent
and I have homework to do.

WATER SHED

As my mother had her toes painted
by the devout Filipina grandmother
she would shout for her little angel
to "get a load of the funny accent"
and ask her what part of Nevada
she hailed from.

Her little angel
wearing bloomers and a fake goatee
would do the next best thing an angel
can do —
besides firing truncated arrows
at mismatched lovers —
I would flutter
my little hummingbird wings
and rising over the beauty parlor
like a carsick cherubim
pee all over the furniture
crash into the gold lamé
spattered mirror.

STEPMOMMY

passing by she could be anybody …
    -Mary Oliver

In another life I would have never
noticed her as she gave me change
at the toll booth, took my order
at Denny's or sold teddy bears
and helium filled balloons
at the hospital shop.
Now she hovers over my dad
like a Swiss guard at the Vatican.
Funny clothes, weapons from
the wrong century, vigilant
eyes watching over someone
already dead.

I suppose
"a poem should have birds in it"
like a peacock calling in a cemetery
like the wife calling my dad to dinner.

PURPLE HEART

Dad's was
self-inflicted
done with the panache
of the desperate.
Instead of two toes
he destroyed his left foot
metatarsals jellied.
He would have shot
his dick off
shot grandpa's dick off
an entire platoon
of grandpas' dicks.

The limp is practically
aristocratic now.
A dueling scar
and the story
varies: shrapnel
as he exposed himself
dragging the biggest piece
of his buddy to safety
mortar fire as he raced forward
guns blazing.

A complex bravery
lighting him
like a Christmas tree.

ROMANCE

He hunts red salmon, chucking "bullfuck" bait
catches black eels that burst teeth on barbed
steel hooks, his feet rotting in the oily brine,
heavy lead peels back from the hull planks
barnacles attach to the corroded wood.

Except for fish I eat no meat, the red-faced man with the
Hansen all-weathers, tubular body and the anger
of Prometheus, lips pressed tight like the
valves of a clam, eats fish only when he hears
Jesus is in the next county.

I look for such men at all the ports o' call
standing stern into dark weather
and remember the rock cod, halibut,
roughy and swordfish, and I never eat any meat now —
nothing at all.

Was it 13 when she first had sex for money
screaming into her fist
teeth marks across her knuckles?
Dad nods when I ask.
He is quiet, as if he is wise
looking like Joseph as his sons return with the silver.
Something happened
it's not the money
but what it had not bought.

No daughter filled with grandchild,
no handsome suitor meeting him with firm hand.
Instead he has paid for silence.
His shoulders do not even shrug,
his palms do not spread open in supplication;
he is simply silent and colored like the end of autumn.

In spite of my Dad's insistence
I don't buy the proud lips of Chopin
tensed over the keyboard as he pounded out
little smiles and family disappointment.
I would rather see flecks of spittle
from the Queen Mother
despoiling the ermine and purple robes,
those always worn at Christ's ascension.
I'm attracted to the droopy-assed Sancho Panza
trailing his lunatic charge
the accumulated steel weapons clanging
like kitchen pots in his burlap sack.
The nitwit Don Quixote
falls off his horse disturbing Zubarran
who is just finishing a still life with desiccated fruit
in the windmill's attic.
The brush pulls hard
across the just glazed canvas.

I turn a smoking page to find St. George
immolated by the dragon.
A satisfied grin spreads across her scaly face
as she sizes me up with green-fire eyes
and from a chapter deep in the middle ages
trumpets sound, a chain mailed hand beckons,
a drawbridge is lowered, horse hooves pound.
Next door a red tricycle drips rusty water

onto a cobblestone road
built by a Roman phalanx with rubber swords.
It is said they built it
to vacation on the Côte d'Azur.

Near appendix A, visiting penguins
are caught helping Joan of Arc
burn religiously in a festooned courtyard.
My mind wanders to blackened Ahi
at the Inn of the Seventh Ray.
Penelope's mother declares *dinner*
ready at the top of her lungs.

I close the book on creaking hinges,
millennia crash together
as I go to wash my hands.
Ulysses is joining us again
more stories without pictures.
I bet Dad is stealing
up behind the wizened bore
frying pan raised, the Ottoman empire
glinting in his eyes.

DELI

Her face knew before she did:
she couldn't have the kosher dill
crunchy and covered with hot mustard,
her teeth dead in her mouth
half her face a sleepy frown.

We ordered the lox plate
egg and garlic bagels,
thick sliced tomatoes and onions,
whipped cream cheese, Jewish and soft.

She was forced to eat daintily
noticing her food like a poet,
her one good hand elegant in its motions,
her frozen right side, watching
like a dead twin.

She has one tooth and hangs her head
like she's worked a field of rice or a factory
floor for 35 years. She orders the pastrami
on a Kaiser roll with a side of
German potato salad.
I cut the sandwich into bite-size pieces,
she picks at the sides of the meat,
looks away from anyone
who could look at her.
This deli is no longer fun.

The numbing pain of rotted gums and nerves
drifts past the table, interjecting bursts
of inky silence.
I listen for Mom's little wheeze
and check silverware for spots,
watch the middle-aged couple in the booth
eat chicken noodle soup from a silvered tin.
A half chicken corpse,
puckered, wan, floats in egg noodles,
long boiled carrots fished
out and examined.

Connoisseurs of carrots so close to my table
the couple is forensic in their exploration.
My mother's strong left hand props up her head
as she looks at the Formica table top,

brown and scratched, her reflection muffled
easy to take in.
While the sandwich sits on her plate
her body sits in the wheelchair
her words sit in her head,
we smile through each other
the desire for somewhere else
spread before us like dessert.

IT EVEN COMES OUT HER EARS

Normally stingy with her urine
she would release it
heartily as she smoked one of Rick's joints

coughing like a cancer patient sneaking a cigarette
her head seemed to close in on itself
squeezing the smoke and wheezes
through her lips and nose

the yellow liquid wets the blue metal
wheelchair, the concrete in the groomed
courtyard staining,
laughter between the hacking fits.

Mother is an abstract term
a belief as easy as falling asleep,
as difficult as my Mom
making the joint hiss
in the liquid at her feet.

ALL THE TEETH KNOCKED OUT OF MOM'S MOUTH, TA DA

I conjure jellyfish and lint,
blow my nose onto a white
silk handkerchief, steady myself
with a collapsing cane.
I look terrible in tails
and patent-leather shoes.
For my last trick a smallish
cage is wheeled onto the stage
by Grandma Lena, sparkling
in a rhinestone halter.

The illusion is simple:
I am placed in the wire apparatus
a six-foot cylinder of chicken
wire is wrapped in cotton,
the door is left open,
I am given 75 years to escape
while Grandma Lena bakes
chocolate chip cookies
with walnuts in a kitchen
stage left. Audience members
are allowed a bathroom break
although no one leaves.

GATHERING

A pigeon-sized balloon
protruding from your head
is desperate, beautiful
and you can still manage Bach
on the harpsichord
with a few botched notes,
play your kids to a draw
in "Mangoes for the madman"
but in arctic evening sun
it is not so much the pallor
as the idea that it will come.
Your eye that can track
the faint outlines of a comet,
will not be able to recognize
your hand; that you will fail
to understand that breathing out
means breathing in;
and hope is a relay event
and you will be handing off soon.

POSSESSION

1.

There is a lacquer box
red lines with a black
background where my
mother kept her bracelets
and gold rings. She went
on about her Japanese box
brought to her after the war,
the one thing her father
intended for her.
She used to say the Japs
were masters at wooden things
like boxes and the little umbrellas
protecting a Mai Tai made down
at the Polynesian bar where
Mom ordered the Pu Pu platter
just for the sniggering name.

Often she'd coach me
on how to primp my hair
pull it back from my forehead
pull the skin at the corner of my
eyes, making me squint "Japanese."
Her laugh was clean
like the streams that feed into
the main river running

through the temple city of Koyosan
in the mountains outside Osaka
where I saw a Buddhist priest
drink three football players under the table,
sake dribbling from their lips,
nothing but cicadas whirring in
the summer night.

2.

I have a picture of a little Japanese girl
yellow rain boots and dwarfing yellow
umbrella against glistening black pavement.
I can hear the stream trickling
as pines rustle up the valley
and I want everything I ever possessed
to easily fit into her wood and bamboo
lunch box.

I remember Mom filling my own tin
Batman box with baloney sandwiches
and stringed potato crisps.
This is the world Mom allows me.
She prepares the plastic-wrapped cookies
and thermos of milk as carefully as a Noh
actor crying in silence.
This is where I keep my mother's love.

7 out of 10 of you think that gravity works pretty well except over the Caspian sea, that most of us have 2 functioning arms, but that in emergencies we have access to an invisible third, packed away between the shoulder blades, 4 out of 1000 of you think that you will be the 1 that Elvis really wanted (to kiss), while all of you are 1 in a million, another 7 out of 10, think Saddam was piloting the jet that went into the north WT tower and that my grandmother was the kindest person on earth, 1 out of 2 of my parents can talk in complete sentences and doesn't wear a diaper, another 1 out of 2 of my parents would not have stopped the slash of his knife over Isaac's throat, no matter if 6 out of 10 Gods of our fathers commanded him.

3 out of 32 million will know someone who has won a lottery, using the money to help amputate invisible limbs, 2 out of 2 of my brothers have been reported as being shanghaied by Malaysian pirates, I'm told that they are doing well, (with 3% error) and according to the most recent statistics, a majority of people in the southern hemisphere will never warm to the idea that a fork and a spoon can ever be successfully combined. For my part, there is only scant evidence, (see Figure 3) with a probability of less than 1 chance in 10,000 that I will know when I will have kissed for the last time or told someone I loved them with the fervor of the newly diagnosed (see Table 2a).

I ONLY LOOKED OUTSIDE

through a window
from the kitchen
elbow on the breakfast table
between half finished plates,
I saw frozen wood cormorants
dip to the winter ground.

These were alive
she told me once,
her eyes wounded black.
I felt my skin like clothing
wrinkle at her touch.

SURFACE

At a time of night when the drunks are asleep
I write and stare at the ends of my body
act on the desire to manipulate marking things
goading them to scratch in some pattern
that tells me this is beautiful,
not fatigue seeping
into my fingertips
depositing an inky dew
on any clean surface.

ENCASED BY LIGHTENING BUGS

She illuminates the smell of roses,
balances pennies on her brow,
freshens her feces with a waved hand
tells me, as the electric motor on the train fails
that we are normal in a hairless world,
dunks her broken thumb in my
cup of cocoa, lets her wig slip,
arranges the makeup of the old woman
with a toothbrush and a Brillo pad,
rips the name tag
off the Mormon kid's wrinkled white shirt
yells, just before they come
We are all God in a child's eye
and these nuns with brisket hands
step up the stairs, habits purplish
in the neon lights, yelling for this woman's
bones, *The crematorium is my empty womb.*
Eggplant and olive oil spill at her feet
pheasants are stamped into the pretty station
tile, the axles of railroad cars half buried
in the mud, a wrought iron entryway
and our marriage certificate fished from
the settling pond.
We leave on West 45th, her arm
in mine, with Windex, buckets
and mops, traffic pauses;
there is a city to be erased.

ANIMIST

She wanted the young man in the thong
the way she did in '64 at Reynold's beach
with the cement breakwater and oily sand.
She knew this in an instant
the smell of a hot dog on-a-stick
just a few particles of food in her nose
more kick than a 30-ot-6
and this was the sound of her metal
walker on the hard wood of the boardwalk
like a shell being scraped out, like a wind
blowing through a bombed-out house.

COLD CALL

After the morning is simply killed
a rising mist, a lone peacock on a cairn,
I think of you in a tight dress, and in ill temper.
These are your lips and flaming hair.
This is my best effort —
I pine like a fool.

This is my wrinkled hand, my lidded stare,
my cracked, tired laugh
as you push me drooling out the door.
I get hard like a porn star
think this is a good, a superlative date,
recite Goethe as I walk circles.

I see no trouble, no absolute rift
you are anger, throb of vestigial
love, this is my life's little secret
kinked mercy, like the Dodo
flightless, extinct.

DRIVING WITH BOTH HANDS ON THE PEANUT BUTTER CUPS

Before I hit the rabbit, I fucked the woman with the goats
and the inconceivable boredom of her children weighing on
her like a planet. The rabbit was dead immediately
body warm as her inner thigh as I dumped it on
the side of the road.

My car does not show dirt or blood and I will go
many weeks before washing it, the turkey buzzards
will be discrete, under the shade tree as they make
quick work of the young rabbit, still somewhat cute
and springy in that child's way.
I poked at its feet expecting it to right itself
and jump away, like a cartoon character,

and I also felt relief that I fucked the woman
before I hit the rabbit, retaining a proper enthusiasm
that resulted in simultaneous orgasms and there are old
fall leaves, a bed, if you will, where I laid the rabbit
softly. But this is after sex and I felt
bad enough about that to make sure that I had told
the rabbit how sorry I was for this.

I would have driven away, perhaps a few words of regret
then back to the AM talk show, and I wasn't really sure
which incident needed more of an apology, the long drive
makes me woozy, the hands of the woman roaming me
like a line of ants, pictures of her children watching us fuck

in bunk beds covered in bright pictures from art class
the eyes of little stick figures glowing at me, but I
prefer to think of the rabbit's regal little pile of bones
and fur, staring at nothing, like a cathedral saint as the
blood made a discrete little halo against the road.

This is the iconography I can worship on all fours:
blood in and out of a body.
The sacred desecrations of adultery and artless murder
make me hungry. I search through paper wrappers
for something sweet to eat.

SEEN NOT HEARD

She has her child riding sidesaddle
across her hip and her breasts
are out the side of her halter
there are photos of a couple
spread all over the house
there are water colors of the photos
of the same couple and a picture
of a dog and a needle point
of the picture of the dog
beside a t-shirt with a photo
of the couple that is on the mantle.
There are bunk beds and raggedy dolls
and finger paintings stuck to the walls with tape.
She takes the baby's hand
points it at me
shapes the fingers into a silent
fuck you, which was our secret sign,
the one that meant *fuck you*
and I'd call the police again
which was also printed on
the t-shirt the baby is wearing.

PAST COOL BLUE FLASHES, A BOMB SQUAD TAKES UP POSITION

I tell you this is the grammar and discipline of boredom.
Reflect on the table surface, scuffed, and not lit by
the west-facing window.
There is a vase with dried field flowers
ambiguous violet and rust, thorny leaves,
autumn vegetables on the sills,
the uneven hardwood floor
is wet with soapy cleaner,
a sharp sweet smell
and the whirring of an ice machine.

The river flowing cold over the three-step falls,
your eyes deep set, light blue, you are aquiline
and pose the question *why this?*
There is rummaging in the walk-in refrigerator,
metal scraping metal, glasses tinkling
against each other, racked for washing.
I am wearing black with black socks and shoes,
eat a chocolate torte with fresh whipped cream,
clear the crumbs from my lap
and see a woman quietly talking to herself,
the empty chairs around her
the dog sleeping at the farthest corner
all now in sunlight, dust motes sparking.
I dance a little salsa sitting,
only my feet shuffling
wonder at nothing.

I notice my fingernails are dirty and jagged
ask myself why it's been so long
this sitting.
My eyes search for the next thing
and then another.

RUSH

The Hungarian dowager
with a dirty fur watches
the lights change
at the corner closest
to the freeway
lurking in the shadows
of the switching
box, a hundred
butterflies or the shade
of Attila looms opalescent
armor-clad,
kindred twitches of light
rush to the woman,
wrap her like a black
flame, the lights
go out
on the avenue,
rock doves are scooped
out of the air by peregrines,
a splash of blood
ruins her pink suede
pumps, the woman
with Penelope's profile
tells her cabby
the Mongol horde
and step on it.

SIMULTANEOUS TRANSLATION

Aggressive like butter she tells me
muy bravo, muy bravo
and I am thinking of the movie
where John Wayne kills 16 million
Indians with 6 bullets,
not Doña Margarita's husband
backhanding her oldest daughter,
bad rum and vomit smelling up the room.
She wrinkles her nose, my Spanish
seems to be improving;
I know most of the words
and could tell her that the weather is
never a good omen, the cat seems to be on fire
and that I like my martini dry.
She nods as she continues washing
clothes, and tells me that her children
hate her for staying with him,
her oldest daughter has never had sex
and that I am a good and kind man.
I assure her in my frayed Castilian
of my rectitude in seducing a woman
with threats of abandonment and scorn,
my hatred for my gentle hands
and ingenuous eyes
is successfully conveyed
to the Doña as is my love
of my flagrant little cock.

34

We nod as one,
wasps build a nest
above our heads, Doña Margarita
finds a female scorpion in my shorts,
cuts it in half with a garden shovel.
Pressing the subjunctive I tell her
that unlike tomorrow
this will be the best of all days.

PATTERN RECOGNITION

Figure eights in the sand crafted
by a tank driven by a 21-year-old
from eastern Kentucky
still growing his mom thinks
all that food he puts away
his long gangly frame
he barely fits into the race car seat
and there are figure eight contrails
in the sky above my house,
large wispy constructions at 50,000 feet,
people look up as I do.

Near the bakery co-op with the notice board
full of guitar teachers and spiritualists
the recycled newspaper box has scare headlines
going on about war
like it has just been invented
and I hear almost nothing
as the wispy figure eights
are spread across the sky
into something that the veterans
down at the barbershop might
mistake for weather.
Farther down the coast
a thermonuclear device makes electricity
for my shaver and toaster.

I'm not as sad as I should be that
I will never get to skid around
a desert in a tank and begrudge
the skinny boy behind the wheel little.
I hit a few tennis balls against
the wall in the gorgeous afternoon light
watch the now straight contrails
for a moment interrupted by the pretty
Asian girl articulately executing
figure eights in her shiny blue Land Rover
she talks on her cellphone
as she whipsaws the leather-covered wheel 180 degrees
a figure eight smile intruding on her
face like a pre-dawn bombing.

THE ONE WHO ANSWERS THE DOOR

She was at the door with spandex and leather,
high boots and long fingers.
My hand was held out to her from a body clad
in torn gym shorts and a dirty Monster truck shirt.
The cough was only for effect.

I told her I needed a moment to put on my face
to imagine a planet where a beautiful woman
you have never met comes to your door
offering you her hand.

I sat on the toilet
trying to imagine myself in such a situation:
how tall would I need to be, which law firm
would I be on the verge of partnering in,
when my next movie would be released.
I replayed the handshake
tried to estimate the width of her smile,
whether she noticed the cat pee smell,
the photos of roadkill I had leaning on the mantel.

What would I need to do to have a woman
with wavy hair and the shoulders of a trapeze
artist, knock on my bathroom door,
ask me
if it's okay.

When they are exposed
there are creases, like chevrons,
on the sides of her breasts.
I suppose these protuberances
had "time in"
assumed a military bearing
are to be saluted,
always at attention.

The efficiency is compelling.
These are breasts
the way God would have wanted them
if he were a man.
Or perhaps, these are breasts for the ages
the saline sacks found
with the bottom jaw
and a few ribs
ten thousand years into the future.
The technology stunning,
after all that time
the plastic sack still resilient and soft
like an India rubber ball
or a leather flight jacket.

LESSON

She held her thumb, middle finger and forefinger
to her nipple.
Like this, roll it back and forth, let the ring finger wander
but not too far, it firms up under use, supports the motion
of the other fingers, you work them against each other.
She holds the chopsticks and closes the ends gently
on a pea, *You can be very precise*, she presses
the secure pea onto the hood of her clit.
The fingers are almost forgotten
there is the hard wood, the pea, and her flesh
something will give.

40

AT SEA

There is little to say when
we disappear from our bodies.
Mindful of this I watch the girlfriend
vanish into her anger.
She registers her hunger
by little teeth marks
in the throw pillow.
She knows her mortality
is as dense as the dust on her shelves;
without tears she tells me
I'm the prison of her love
we are made only for each other
like the hemlock cup and Socrates' lips.

Instead I see her
like Frankenstein's monster
alone on a broken ship in the Arctic
while her shrouded figure
looms at the mast.
Creaking wood and the gurgle of water,
a finished journal losing its ink
in the heavy air.

FOOD INSTEAD OF ALLEGORY

The woman who you want to see
is wearing a bird
walking on pumps made of dictionaries
where all the adjectives
have been transformed into "yowsa."
There are these high windmills
that have the face of this woman
printed on every sail.
The Dutch accents are lost
behind her billowing nose.
You sit in the choir
smelling like an Italian kitchen
and smile as the dishes of esoteric foods
are passed between the pews.
Now comes the disagreement
also passed between the pews,
smashed crockery and the woman
you have almost seen
is wrinkling her nose at smelly babies
and having her bird fly off
and the dictionaries strapped to her feet
peck at her like badly trained Pekingese.
This is the official story:
the man will recount his flavor,
the dictionary will find a poet
and the bird will be shot from the sky.

REPARATIONS

I drag a foot across rubble
stay right between my eyes
and with stiff fingers
scratch my name in the dust.

I tell her that Vukovar will
shake itself awake
like Brigadoon
or Shiva's one hundred-year blink.

In a Mandela of still drying bones
I read to her figments of our lovely
past, palms un-cracked, eyes
clear enough to see
peeling lips
as the fresh bloom of a rose
or the smiles
and uneven teeth of two lovers
stamping each other sexless.

Almost women turn to page 22
Virgins ask directions
how to eat ice cream.
Are Italian men into Crisco?
Paranoia test on page 45
makes me think
magazine is tapped.
Girls with large breasts
write poems (bare all)
page 54. Body poll finds
belly button rings
rad sexy.

Monica pulls me
mumbling from the newsrack
suggests *Golden Showers*
is to the left.
I sense a distance
develop, decide to eat more
low fat chocolate
be attentive to her needs
cultivate a more mature demeanour
just like Fantasy Lover
page 63.

ON A FARM (OR SOMEWHERE ELSE)

She had to go into overwhelming detail
about the day she tripped and crushed
the back of her calico kitten, it didn't die
suddenly, hadn't done anything more abnormal
than run for a yarn ball from the winter wool
K's dead father (shoelaces, tractor) had spun.
But the death of the kitten
was different, one moment curious and with a whole
lifetime of cat to turn into, the next, writhing
and slowly losing consciousness
which even for a cat is something to hold closely.
K tossed this off as another barnyard casualty
like I did her father
but this is where I start with the tears.

I am not a villain or scrofulous psychopath
confusing a human with a girl's beginning pet
the tapping little paws of a 2-month-old kitten
but the bare face of death has many wrinkles
and K's father's bubbles up in dreams,
her voice is his, her whimpers split his smile
or it's the wind instead of a subtle meow
or the soft brush of wool.

FALSE ANALOGY

I want her the way I want health
never-ending, obligatory and fair.
I want her without the words
without the headache of successfully attaching myself
like breading to chicken.
This plain and visual relation is easy
enough, but her words run too thick against me
pulling away in large sheets,
she is consistent and has facility and grace
the frilly behavior that lies on her like a thin film.
I am afraid of such facile connections;
we do not cook the way we make love,
we do not thrill to the simple strips of similarities
that bind, unbind, and flour is not a film of sweat
earning its presence, its purity
by the rubbing together of our skin,
the clear failure, the features of erotic despair.

WHAT THE POET DOES

It's not that he wants to be like Bukowski
looking for his teeth near the bar's toilet,
vomiting in the Geraniums,
but he likes his drink, not to assuage the fear of death
or the simple anxiety of flying, he likes the taste,
doesn't have a problem with waking up to a headache
the size of a small Italian city, and isn't overly bothered
by being too drunk to find his way home on certain
warm nights when anyone
would want to be out under the stars.

That one of those times was last night
is neither here nor there.
It was a little difficult to get to sleep
wedged between the empty
aluminum beer barrels behind the ski lodge
but not different enough
from lying awake in bed worrying
about the placement of commas
in the broken sestina about his wife's miscarriage;
it's not the miscarriage (her third) that was the problem
but the poetry implicit in these events
requiring such a difficult form.

I understand this completely
the challenge is not the mourning
or even the demands of some obscure piling on of lines

or being soberly housed
in fact, he likes the taste and the stars,
the roof of trees and the silence spread out around him
like a hushed audience readying him to begin.

Thin ice, he said, winding himself up like a crossbow,
shifting his crossed legs to the left in the cane chair,
his torso with his folded arms moving to the right.
You're on it and he added a toothy
my friend and I thought of a little girl in a yellow wool
coat skating on the pond near the city center, slow trout
and bass in the winter water, worry wrinkles forming
the ice bowing in like an old mattress.

I'm not sure if she manages to get by this danger or force
herself through the surface or else it opens up to her like a
questionable uncle with bad teeth, let's say she goes in,
perhaps the water is shallow, she's soaked up to her knees
scrambles out yelling bloody murder. Or it's deep
like Convict Lake early spring, her friends come to her
with rope, fish her out, get her to the car, heater set to high,
teeth chattering, a close call, is that what thin ice is?

Thin ice, a call for help, rescuers arrive, succeed
or fail, and in this failure lose themselves in the gunmetal
water. A little girl spins figures on a shiny surface, white
patent-leather skates, pigtails and training bra, she turns
fast enough to drill through the ice
or fly up on broken sunlight.

My friend could be inviting me to skate deeper onto
the brittle surface. It's not only the moment when I start out
but the final crack as I am thrown into the cold,
limbs going numb, people running.

EXTRUDED THROUGH MY EYES

I wish he would spontaneously combust,
a little puff of smoke interrupting
his 18th heroic couplet, "the mystery
of the universe" left dangling in
the sulphurous air,
a swatch of singed black cloth
drifting to the floor.

I want the four riders of the
apocalypse to thunder onto the stage,
carry him off in little bits,
rejections slips
in pink and yellow
fluttering like Monarch butterflies
as they gallop past.

I need his
broken metaphors
to escape
from the podium,
run for the exits
leaving only fragrant
curses echoing
in our ears.

NICE LIKE DEATH

The legs are covered in black stretch cotton
from her snakeskin cowboy boots to her thighs
stovepipes, her blouse red satin flows away from her
like smoke released in a poisonous burning, she pulls
her poems from a wicker envelope,
smiles with translucent teeth
and there is her voice: smooth and hushed, a stage
whisper, a winking sigh, beautiful syllables pile up
like decorative pillows, a place for the damned to
rest their heads.

Never looking up
the man with thick biker boots
Airborne tattoo and yellow legal pad
unkinks arms and cracks knuckles
bends low to the table
dots top left corner of pad
with red felt marker
watched with professional approval
by the white-haired bearded drifter
drinking Calistoga mineral water
on the Light House terrace.

Fire engines take route #89 to tree fire.
Forest Service Air Marauder flies in low,
with a deep chortle releases purple retardant
bombing last flames.
Safeway checker on break
takes a good look,
lights her Camel
while a tanker circles around,
flies off low across Carnellian Bay.
I remember a squadron delivering napalm
at camp Cao Yi Dong, cry as lobstered tourists
drip ice cream on well-protected lawns.

OBJET D'ART

There is this kid next to me
two months after suicided father
and I have this goddamn orange harmonica to write about
and the kid is rhyming a 100,000 drachma note
and his shoelaces are hanging down from his shoes
like walrus whiskers and I'm trying to notice everything.

This world is not the world of a fatherless child
who plays with a worthless banknote and has the dreams
of someone else's father rousing him from sleep.
Making sure there is a collar sticking out from his sweater
this is the object I will keep by my hands
keep in sight — the child/father with his alligator shoes
tousled hair and a neon orange harmonica.

Over my baked Alaska and heirloom mushrooms
through a crack in the mountain wall
it looked like Moses was having another
conversation with God.
All I could hear was the guy at the next table
go on about tax law while K was telling me
that her boss was without a large penis
and from what I could tell it looked like the beefy
casino employees in the parking lot were elbowing
each other and laughing at the caged white tiger.
This tiger was two beefy employees long
and opened its cartoon mouth as if to roar.
What came out was the laugh of the accountant
from Cincinnati — I suppose something like a roar —
and I nibbled at the chocolate chip cheesecake
watched the cat continue its turns as the men
lost interest and the forklift moved heavy boxes
working toward the tiger destined for a magician's
cheesy disappearing act.
In the distance there was a pine valley
of Jurassic parody — low mist and chiaroscuro —
stretching out into a moonless night. Below
the parking lot was filling with dark
and the scuttling of security guards.
The tiger had been put away with the rest of the act:
costumes, stage lifts, dull guillotines
and rubber sabers.

ARC LIGHT

The deep rust leaves along the trail
leading to the waterfall
tile the ground explicitly
as if every leaf was placed by hand
then adjusted for effect.
My eyes track the light
and upward slope
species of tree are passed in silence.
My interest in the differences
between Witch Hazel and Heather
is still dormant.
I catch the contrails of a B-52 bomber
fifty-thousand feet in the air
a Euclidean cloud
two parallel marks
pure white against the thinning canopy
of what have to be autumn Maples.

I know what that bomber is
beyond the naming —
its contents of 20 two-thousand-pound cluster bombs
six air-to-ground cruise missiles
stowed precisely
its crew of six
trained to symphonic destruction
navigation, fire control, bombardier, pilot.

I know the functions of flight suits
the fuel capacity of a fully loaded plane.

They cannot see me —
in the trees by the three-tongued waterfall
monarch butterflies dancing through the sumac —
at five-hundred miles-per-hour.
They see in large sweeps of horizon
understand the inside of phrases:
"enemy degradation, attrited capacity, collateral damage"
and they sleep restfully in leather chairs.

Some people know every plant they ever see
poisons to be used or avoided
the condition of soil
how the weather might come hard.
I need to know tax law and use flower names
to gussy up a poem.
As I condense into ink spots
real answers arrive in rapid thumps
the blows of exact description
a two thousand pound bomb
blasts upward and to the side
concussion the only form of action
shrapnel useless against buildings
the thin-walled, tear-shaped containers
leave nothing behind.

BLOOD RED THAT ISN'T BLOOD

I will casually leave out my inarticulate screaming
at the 80-year-old woman who brings me lukewarm
Turkish coffee, or my fits of vomiting when I hear
the F-16s dive into another bombing run,
no I will give you acts of overcoming
rising from my weakness to pull a child
out of harm's way.
Large caliber bullets ripping at me as we run
each moment broadening into a chapter
of my new poetry book.
I will make my troubled sleep
turn into something as deep as shrapnel
buried in the wall of a children's center.
I will see colors more vividly
as if I have the eyes of a thousand parrots
smell cinnamon in the breath of all people
not blood dried to a fine red dust.
I will tend lovingly to the family of the dead;
embarrassing in this exsanguination
my cowardice is sealed here.

SHAHEED

His picture was pasted to the living room wall
The mother smiled with her daughter on the couch
Omar ate pita and chicken with Zatar
I stared at the 50-caliber machine gun holes

The mother smiled with her daughter on the couch
The Merkava tank gunned its engines, spewing smoke
I stared at the 50-caliber machine gun holes
Omar said his brother was too young to blow up

The Merkava tank gunned its engines, spewing smoke
A parakeet twittered by the kitchen door
Omar said his brother was too young to blow up
The mother was crying as her daughter sang

A parakeet twittered by the kitchen door
The soldier was coming up the stairs
The mother was crying as her daughter sang
He was young, about the same age

The soldier was coming up the stairs
A Tom and Jerry cartoon was going manic on TV
He was young, about the same age
We all watched the mouse smash the cat with a nailed club

His picture was pasted to the living room wall

NOT ME IN NABLUS

I wasn't the boy shot through the hand
as he walked along Sal-hedin street
idly brushing his fingers against the concrete market stalls.
His hand, not mine
would sometimes throw rocks at the tanks
smoking up the streets near the school.
I wasn't the girl with the scraped knees
and circular rubber bullet bruises
cornered by a jeep as she returned home;
and how could I be my uncle
hung by his feet in Ariel
until blood bloated and blushed his head.
Nor am I the blasted body of a mother
cut in half by her bedroom door
as soldiers triggered a shaped charge.

The differences are obvious:
my hands are whole
and I use them to make Italian pastry chefs,
British pensioners, and French jugglers laugh
at my pantomime of soldiers hiding in tanks
shooting at my friends with shirts on their heads.
A hundred feet away a sniper
runs his laser across someone's chest.
How could it be my chest?
It is not my heart and lungs blasted away
by a tumbling 25-caliber shell

It is not my blood running out my mouth
and it is not my smile stuck to my face
like a paper donkey's tail.
I am still telling this story
an insightful, and more to the point, living narrator
who lets you believe death
is for someone else
in some other place.

SOAKED BY GOD

I wanted a blessing for the children
I saw burning tires by the burnt-out
VW on the street in Ramallah
where army tanks marked the road
like a pack of dogs.
The children throwing stones
could be casting flowers on the waters
of some sacred river where the petals
pull apart, flowing into the sea,
a sea said to feed God's tears
but the stoning was casual.
Like the casting off of Esau's birthright
they were casting off childhood
and this was a deception accepted like Isaac's
boneheaded confusion.
The children in tanks
and the children with t-shirts
tied on their heads, throwing rocks,
could have been switched by any half-witted
God and no one would have been the wiser
but even such gods seem to —
as some random rule of almighty behavior —
allow themselves one chance.
Like only being allowed six days
to create the world
or eating Jell-O with your hands
tied behind your back.

So the kids in badly arranged Kaffiyehs
and those with Kevlar vests
played out this game
while God gets lime-flavored Jell-O
all over his helpless face.

HOMER AT THE HOT DOG STAND

Chafing, raw, reddened skin
from friction the man tells me
all chicken fried and coated with sun.
I'm surrounded by him
like the atmosphere of a dying planet.
He was here before mathematics
before the first winter collecting
so many layers of blue
or before a brother had teeth large
enough to kill his twin.
I had little on offer
simply considered splitting the Pringles
and Slurpees, too shell-shocked to talk
or to feed my child the last little dollup
of Gerber's yams.
The man was all sepulchral
as he described a war drenched in red sunsets
a "blood red that is not blood"
or of the mountain of three goddesses
sans goddesses.
He shakes his head as my child screams
Do you charge for that baby?
he winks, the baby starting to hum
not like an opera singer
but like a washing machine
something to calm the parents.

Even after all this
there is a singing about paradise.

MARRIAGE TRICK

Birthday parties were always
a parent's nightmare.
Children would watch him
slash his wrists,
dismember a rabbit,
never quite cut through
the volunteer.
All to be revealed as an illusion
the pulsing artery,
a clever ruse
the crimson limbs
plastic and soft.

Not convinced
his wife wanted him
to disappear
vanish himself into some
cheerful heap of little red and yellow
silk handkerchiefs
and to use a chainsaw
or a solid wooden bench
on his exaggerated
young assistant.

SUSHI

I wanted to ask
the man what sustained
his little girl's delight
his floppy dog-eared
smile as she
poured her Coke
all over the
well-presented
California roll.

Butterflies blossomed
from the bubbles
flying past our table,
chopsticks parallel
wasabi coloring
small china plates.

WHERE IT ENDS

We frighten
our children simply
forgetting the time
or quoting ourselves
again and again.

After a month
two centuries
or the argument
your hair would turn white
teeth would yellow
and the dog's tail
would drop to the floor.

If a choir were to answer
baritones and breathy
sopranos, something
to carry to your coffin
in cupped hands
a potato and persimmon corsage.

Nudged toward arctic light
the touch of granite
or a tumor
I go directly for this thing
a dog

and a killing hand
we lick the mud off
as if it's love.

THE SAME SIDE OF THE ARGUMENT

You say that there are frogs mating down by
the all-night donut shop across from the park
with lamps lit by short men in black capes, toting step-
ladders and muttering about union dues that give them
nothing but nickel-plated belt buckles.
The detail is astonishing, the precision suspect,
there are magpies with fidgety calls
heavy trucks chewing at garbage lining the streets,
a woman with tattoos on one side of her body
distressed about clothes that show her non-indelibly
marked skin which would not have been
the case just a few years earlier, but again, fashion,
like a half-eaten burrito
has little credibility in a place where tongues
are regularly torn from mouths
and butterflies drizzle to earth
half-dead with nostalgia and ennui.
I claim these latter two must be responsible
and not the earth's atmosphere
senile in its attempts to cover the planet
in something other than the vacuum of space.

ACKNOWLEDGEMENTS:

I am grateful to the publishers and editors of the following periodicals and publications, in which some of the poems in this book first appeared:

Echo 681
Interbang
Jacaranda Review
King Log
Parthenon West
Shades of Contradiction
The Squaw Valley Review
Texas Observer

I am also grateful to the Vermont Studio Center for support during the time when the manuscript of this book was in preparation.

This book would never have been possible without the critical eye, encouragement and loving badgering of Kathryn Dowling, she is my own private peanut gallery.

MARQUIS

MEMBER OF SCABRINI GROUP

Québec, Canada
2006

3 1143 00926 1562